"With theological richness and devotional warmth, Josh Moody guides us through Advent as he walks us through the Gospel accounts of the greatest story ever told. Your heart will be stirred and your mind enriched as your eyes are pointed to the child of the manger and the Lord of salvation. Here believers will be drawn afresh into the wonder and joy of the Saviour's arrival – and those just exploring the faith will find a gentle and winsome invitation to experience that same wonder and to discover that unmatched joy."

**JONATHAN GRIFFITHS,**
Lead Pastor, The Metropolitan Bible Church, Ottawa, Canada

"Christmas is meant to be a time for joy, but the demands of the secular culture and shallowness of superficial sentimentality often mean that we do not experience the joy Jesus should bring. These short, accessible reflections on the gospel stories of the birth of Jesus unpack what these momentous events meant for all the key characters who lived through them, and will renew your joy in the good news of God's grace and sovereign plan of salvation. They are ideal both for personal and family use, with challenging questions for personal application that will allow these wonderful truths to penetrate your heart afresh."

**JOHN STEVENS,**
National Director, Fellowship of Independent
Evangelical Churches (FIEC), UK

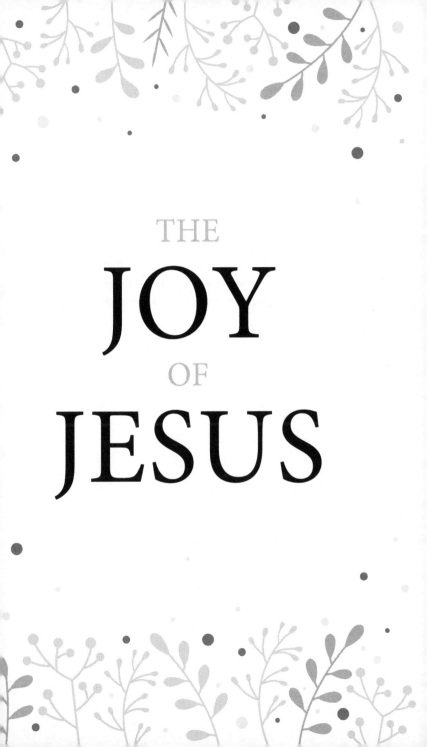

# THE
# JOY
## OF
# JESUS

*For Rochelle,*
*whose idea it was for us to read these Bible*
*passages together each year as a family, and*
*who made the original selection of the verses.*

# THE
# JOY
## OF
# JESUS

## 25 DEVOTIONAL READINGS
## FOR CHRISTMAS

## JOSH MOODY

### CHRISTIAN
### FOCUS

Copyright © Josh Moody 2024

Hardback ISBN: 978-1-5271-1130-1
Ebook ISBN: 978-1-5271-1140-0

10 9 8 7 6 5 4 3 2 1

Published in 2024
by
Christian Focus Publications Ltd,
Geanies House, Fearn, Ross-shire,
IV20 1TW, Great Britain

www.christianfocus.com

Designed and typeset by Pete Barnsley (CreativeHoot.com)

Printed by Gutenberg, Malta

# CONTENTS

# PREFACE

Advent is a season when we celebrate the coming of Christ and look forward with expectation to His second coming!

Each year our family has a tradition of opening one Advent Bible reading starting on December 1 and finishing on Christmas Day, December 25. I am sharing those Bible readings with some thoughts based on them for use as a devotional during this season.

This book is to help us with this joyful sense of wonder. It also functions as a prayerful reminder: to celebrate the real meaning of Christmas. Christmas, at its most basic, is about the gift of Christ to save us from our sins. It speaks of the humility of God. It speaks of the grace of God. It speaks of the peace of God. It speaks of the beauty of the Savior in His infant lowliness reaching down to lift us to His divine loftiness. It means that anyone—anyone from any background, culture or socio-economic bracket, anyone at all, no matter what they have done or said or thought—may rejoice this Christmas!

May your hearts and souls be filled with Christ this Christmas by His Spirit. May you 'taste and see that the Lord is good' (Ps. 34:8). And may, as Isaiah put it, you hear the message of 'comfort, comfort my people' and see the 'glory of the Lord…revealed' (Isa. 40:1,5).

# SHOCKING JOY

*In the sixth month of Elizabeth's pregnancy, God sent the angel Gabriel to Nazareth, a town in Galilee, to a virgin pledged to be married to a man named Joseph, a descendant of David. The virgin's name was Mary. The angel went to her and said, 'Greetings, you who are highly favored! The Lord is with you.'* **(LUKE 1:26-28)**

In Luke's Gospel, the master historian and medical doctor, Luke, records all the facts with care. Like all good storytellers, he also has a taste for the dramatic. It was 'in the sixth month of Elizabeth's pregnancy' that once again God is on the move. He sends an angel to give the most shocking news any young virgin could ever, and would ever, receive. She is highly favored. And the Lord is with her.

This Christmas, would you reflect upon the extraordinary truth of Emmanuel, God with us? That in Christ, God Himself is with us! That as Mary was 'highly favored' to play her extraordinary role in the drama of salvation that first Christmas, so we are now eternally assured of God's loving presence in the midst of heartache, trouble, unexpected pregnancy, pain, or disease.

Mary was not famous. She was not powerful. She was by all the world's standards insignificant. A forgotten person in the middle of a forgotten corner of a far-flung empire. A people who had been in exile, recently returned, and were still under the power of a foreign regime.

To say that she was 'highly favored' was at least counterintuitive, if not downright shocking! But to receive Christ this Christmas is to be part of this great high favor of having God Himself with us. How amazing it is that people like you and me (and Mary) can be recipients of God's high favor! How extraordinary that the lowly, the ignored, the marginalized, the forgotten, the small and (apparently) insignificant can play such a pivotal part in the drama of God's salvation! How wonderful it is that God is *with us*, the God of all grace and comfort. To have God with us, this God, this God of love and favor, is a truth that can feel almost too good to be true. How can it be? How can someone like Mary, someone like me or you, experience God's personal presence with us? And yet, at Christmas we remember *God with us*. And we not only remember, we also have the opportunity to receive. To receive *Him*, to know the very presence of God, to encounter Jesus, this Emmanuel. Amazing but true, wonderful, extraordinary, stunning, shocking joy.

Reflect on the great Christmas carol 'O Come, O Come, Emmanuel' at the start of Advent:

> *O come, O come, Emmanuel*
> *And ransom captive Israel*
> *That mourns in lonely exile here*
> *Until the Son of God appear.*
> *Rejoice! Rejoice! Emmanuel*
> *Shall come to thee, O Israel.*

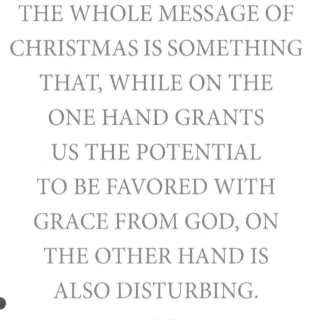

"

THE WHOLE MESSAGE OF
CHRISTMAS IS SOMETHING
THAT, WHILE ON THE
ONE HAND GRANTS
US THE POTENTIAL
TO BE FAVORED WITH
GRACE FROM GOD, ON
THE OTHER HAND IS
ALSO DISTURBING.

(p.9)

# TROUBLING JOY

*Mary was greatly troubled at his words and wondered what kind of greeting this might be. But the angel said to her, 'Do not be afraid, Mary, you have found favor with God. You will conceive and give birth to a son, and you are to call him Jesus. He will be great and will be called the Son of the Most High. The Lord God will give him the throne of his father David, and he will reign over Jacob's descendants forever; his kingdom will never end.'*

*'How will this be,' Mary asked the angel, 'since I am a virgin?'* **(LUKE 1:29-34)**

Now the angel's greeting had left Mary disturbed, deeply and profoundly concerned. While many of us might have been pleased to have been told by an angel that we are highly favored, the consistent witness of Scripture is that when someone meets an angel they are scared. Far from the childhood picture of an angel as a sweet little fairy, angels appeared to people in the Bible as terrifying visitations. So, the angel notices that, like so many times when they appear to humans, Mary is frightened by the sight of an angel.

But not only is Mary afraid at the very sight of an angel, she is worried about being told that she is highly favored. What on earth (or in heaven) could be going on? Why is she being selected of all the people she knew for this kind of greeting? Contrary to popular belief, even in the Bible, angelic appearances are extremely rare. And when they occur, it is not common to be told immediately that you are highly favored. Mary, greeted in this high and lofty manner, shows her humility by being troubled by it, not being puffed up by it.

Then the angel explains. This thing that is going to happen is absolutely and completely miraculous. You have found favor with God. You will have a child, called Jesus, who will be great and the Son of the Most High. He is in the line of David, and He will rule from David's throne. God's kingdom is coming! And, Mary, you are going to have an absolutely key part to play in this divine drama.

Once again, Mary shows her character. She is not only humble, she is level-headed. Hold on here, 'I am a virgin, how can this be?' And Mary receives an answer (verses 35-37) that for a lesser person would have been unacceptable, but for Mary, highly favored, it was enough that the Lord had spoken (verse 38).

The whole message of Christmas is something that, while on the one hand grants us the potential to be favored with grace from God, on the other hand is also disturbing. That God would come into this world. That God would come to redeem. That God (the 'divine interferer' as C.S. Lewis said he felt about Him in his pre-conversion days) would mess around in our lives, and so break with our so-called rules as to rupture spacetime and invest the magnanimity of deity in a baby. Joy, certainly, but disturbing! The kind of joy that does not allow us to go about our lives in the same old way, in the same old patterns, with the same old temptations to give into, and the same old squabbles to have, the same meaningless lives to lead. No, this great disturber speaks a new dawn of a new day, and its message, if received afresh again this Christmas, will disturb us as it grants the favor of joy forever.

IF ANY PERSON IS A
PERSON TO REMIND US
OF THE POWER OF THE
SEED OF GOD'S WORD,
IT IS THE PERSON AND
STORY OF MARY.

(p.12)

# BIBLICAL JOY

*The angel answered, 'The Holy Spirit will come on you, and the power of the Most High will overshadow you. So the holy one to be born will be called the Son of God. Even Elizabeth your relative is going to have a child in her old age, and she who was said to be unable to conceive is in her sixth month. For no word from God will ever fail.'*

*'I am the Lord's servant,' Mary answered. 'May your word to me be fulfilled.' Then the angel left her.* **(LUKE 1:35-38)**

How is this possible? A simple answer: God is going to do it. Simple, perhaps, but not without verification. The angel points to the astonishing fact, of which Mary was familiar, that Elizabeth was having a child at her advanced age. Contemporary medical science would have predicted that such a birth was, practically speaking, impossible.

Mary's pregnancy was impossible by all medical science ever conceived by man. Yet, nothing is impossible for God. And in pointing to Elizabeth, verification is given to Mary to help her with faith.

But not only that: she is also given a text from the Old Testament which (perhaps?) would also have been familiar to her. Another remarkable birth had been promised, a foreshadow of this far more remarkable one. And the angel's words then were an echo of these: 'Is anything too hard for the Lord?' (Gen. 18:14). If that word had not fallen to the ground, and had not failed, then Mary could be confident that this far greater Word from God would not fail too.

Oh, Christian, trust in God's Word. In the midst of all the tinsel and fairy dust of Christmas, do not get so distracted by the glamour that you forget to even glance at the God whose Word made it all possible, and whose Word was made flesh. If any time of year is a time to remember to read the Bible, it is the time of Christmas. If any person is a person to remind us of the power of the seed of God's Word, it is the person and story of Mary. She who was 'highly favored' was faced with a challenge to her faith greater than any that will ever face any of us. She was graciously given confirmation. And with that evidence before her replied, 'May your word to me be fulfilled' (as the Word had been fulfilled to Sarah so long before).

What time today could you carve out to give to God's Word? What time this week could you utilize for the purpose of hearing God's Word? What promise is there in God's Word that you could today rest upon, knowing 'No word from God will EVER fail'! (Luke 1:37).

"

BLESSED IS SHE WHO
HAS BELIEVED THAT THE
LORD WOULD FULFILL
HIS PROMISES TO HER!

(p.15)

# BLESSED JOY

*At that time Mary got ready and hurried to a town in the hill country of Judea, where she entered Zechariah's home and greeted Elizabeth. When Elizabeth heard Mary's greeting, the baby leaped in her womb, and Elizabeth was filled with the Holy Spirit. In a loud voice she exclaimed: 'Blessed are you among women, and blessed is the child you will bear! But why am I so favored, that the mother of my Lord should come to me? As soon as the sound of your greeting reached my ears, the baby in my womb leaped for joy. Blessed is she who has believed that the Lord would fulfill his promises to her!'* **(LUKE 1:39-45)**

Not being slow to test the truth of that which she had believed, Mary hurries off to find Elizabeth. She had some pretty exciting news to tell her! Two mothers with two extraordinary babies, one more extraordinary than ever before or again. Elizabeth hears Mary's excited shout of greeting, and the baby inside her leaps for joy.

Never having been pregnant myself, it is hard for me to imagine what that must have been like for Elizabeth. I do remember one of our children's little fists suddenly moving across the wall of the womb in such a way that you could see the hand from outside. What would it be like for a baby to 'leap' for joy? Pretty extraordinary. But not only is the future John the Baptist leaping for joy, Elizabeth is also filled with the Holy Spirit. Her filling with the Holy Spirit results in a prophetic exclamation which centers on a triple blessing:

1. Blessed is Mary!

2. Blessed is the child!

3. Blessed is the one who, like Mary did, believes God's promises!

The promise given to Mary was like a tuning fork bringing into song all the spiritually minded within its vicinity. A magnet causing all the magnetized elements of gospel joy to rush towards the receiver of the promises of God with delight!

Are you so moved by the presence of the promises of God? Are you exhilarated by the person of Jesus—more than trends, fashions, tastes and preferences, more than life itself?

For those who respond to the Christ of Christmas with faith ('Blessed is she [or he] who believes that the Lord would fulfill His promises to her [or him]'), there is a thrice pronounced blessing. God declares that this posture of faith towards the Christ of His promise is the zone of the joy of blessing! This Christmas, can you begin to see more of how all your greatest delights are fulfilled in Him?

*Joy to the world! The Lord is come*
*Let earth receive her King!*
*Let every heart prepare Him room...*
*No more let sins and sorrows grow*
*Nor thorns infest the ground*
*He comes to make*
*His blessings flow*
*Far as the curse is found...*

**'Joy to the World'** by Isaac Watts, 1719

> MY SOUL DOTH
> MAGNIFY THE LORD:
> AND MY SPIRIT HATH
> REJOICED IN GOD
> MY SAVIOUR.

(p.21)

# HUMBLE JOY

*And Mary said:*
*'My soul glorifies the Lord*
*    and my spirit rejoices in God my Savior,*
*for he has been mindful*
*    of the humble state of his servant.*
*From now on all generations will call me blessed,*
*for the Mighty One has done great things for me—*
*    holy is his name.*
*His mercy extends to those who fear him,*
*    from generation to generation.*
*He has performed mighty deeds with his arm;*
*    he has scattered those who are proud in their*
*inmost thoughts.*
*He has brought down rulers from their thrones*
*    but has lifted up the humble.*
*He has filled the hungry with good things*
*    but has sent the rich away empty.*
*He has helped his servant Israel,*
*    remembering to be merciful*

*to Abraham and his descendants forever,*
*just as he promised our ancestors.'* **(LUKE 1:46-55)**

The famous 'Magnificat' or Mary's Song is justly well-known for its glorious, heartfelt, profound, and elevating magnification of Christ. It contrasts Him, with His glory and power, with her, in her weakness and frailty. Consider this beautiful line: 'For the Mighty One has done great things for me' (verse 49). And who is this 'me'? She tells us: 'humble state' (verse 48) (read: poor and marginalized and knows it); 'humble' (verse 52) (read: and knows her lowly state all too well); 'hungry' (verse 53) (read: really physically hungry, perhaps, and at least truly desperate). This is the one that the 'Mighty One' had done great things for!

Her song also mirrors an earlier 'promise of [her] ancestors' (verse 55), the prayer of Hannah in 1 Samuel 2. The overlap of theme and spirit is notable. Mary is steeped in Scripture and able to sing in Scripture, too! She recognizes in this moment before her (in her!) a fulfillment of that moment when Hannah who spoke of the anointed one to come.

What a God is this who 'has helped his servant Israel, remembering to be merciful to Abraham and his descendants forever' (verses 54-55)!

Would you then, this Christmas, look not on your 'state,' whether poor or rich, honored or defamed, and instead look to the One who delights in elevating the lowly for the sake of His glory? Would you not rely on your riches— if you have them—and instead rely on Him? And would you, whether male or female, sing along with Mary of the gratuitous grace of the Son of God who came down to earth to rescue His people?

In the old words of the Book of Common Prayer:

*My soul doth magnify the Lord: and my spirit hath*
*rejoiced in God my Saviour.*
*For he hath regarded: the lowliness of his handmaiden.*
*For behold, from henceforth: all generations shall*
*call me blessed.*
*For he that is mighty hath magnified me: and*
*holy is his Name.*
*And his mercy is on them that fear him: throughout*
*all generations.*
*He hath shewed strength with his arm: he hath*
*scattered the proud in the imagination of their hearts.*
*He hath put down the mighty from their seat: and hath*
*exalted the humble and meek.*
*He hath filled the hungry with good things: and the rich*
*he hath sent empty away.*
*He remembering his mercy hath holpen his servant*
*Israel: as he promised to our forefathers, Abraham and*
*his seed for ever.*

"

IF MARY NEEDED
TIME WITH ELIZABETH,
YOU WILL NEED TIME
WITH SOME OTHER
DISCIPLE, TOO.

(p.25)

# COMMUNITY JOY

*Mary stayed with Elizabeth for about three months and then returned home.* **(LUKE 1:56)**

A short reading today! But I love these little human touches that Luke gives us in the midst of his grand narrative. We have just heard the Magnificat. We have had the announcement of the birth of John the Baptist, and of the Christ. We have gloried in the highest heights, and now Luke gives us some domestic details and relational insights. Why?

Luke loves to assure us that the things of which he writes are *true*. He says at the beginning of the Gospel:

*Many have undertaken to draw up an account of the things that have been fulfilled among us, just as they were handed down to us by those who from the first were eyewitnesses and servants of the word. With this in mind, since I myself have carefully investigated everything from the beginning, I too decided to write an orderly account for you, most excellent Theophilus, so that you may know the certainty of the things you have been taught.* **(LUKE 1:1-4)**

In other words, Luke is writing to assure his readers that what they had heard about the Christ is actually, truly, historically credible. Those things truly happened. And he gathers his sources, and tells the old story, with a special lens on its verification as factually accurate. So, he includes these details, these facts, these elements that give the 'ring of truth' as J.B. Phillips famously put it.

But it also tells of the human scale of this moment. Here was this young woman, barely more than a girl, who had received this thunderous news. What does she do? She stays with Elizabeth to get settled. To talk over the things that they had heard. To share together.

Christmas is a factual story. The message of Christmas is a historically verifiable and accurate narrative of the events. It is not subject to the experimental science of a laboratory, but it is subject to the experimental science of the history books. It happened. Luke tells us.

But not only did it happen, there were real people involved. People like you and me who had needs, and desires, and hopes and dreams. What we find here with this little line about the relationship between Elizabeth and Mary is an emphasis of the truth of the story, and an inkling of the relational interweaving of the burgeoning Christian community.

Do you have friends? Do you know people in the church? Do you let others know you? Do you share the joys (and the trials) of life with some other confidant? Who is there who you can call upon in your hour of need, or share with in your hour of elation? Perhaps this Christmas it is time to pray that God would help you join in a discipleship relationship with another fellow traveler down the Christian road, connect with a Bible study, and become involved in a church. If Mary needed time with Elizabeth, you will need time with some other disciple, too.

*O church, arise and put your armor on;*
*Hear the call of Christ your captain;*
*For now the weak can say they are strong*
*In the strength that God has given.*
*With shield of faith and belt of truth*
*We'll stand against the devil's lies;*
*An army bold whose battle cry is 'love!'*
*Reaching out to those in darkness.*

**'O Church Arise'** by Keith Getty and Stuart Townend,
Thankyou Music, 2005

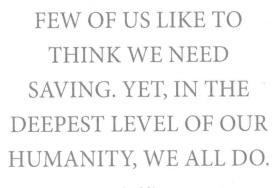

"

FEW OF US LIKE TO
THINK WE NEED
SAVING. YET, IN THE
DEEPEST LEVEL OF OUR
HUMANITY, WE ALL DO.

(p.29)

# SAVING JOY

*This is how the birth of Jesus the Messiah came about: his mother Mary was pledged to be married to Joseph, but before they came together, she was found to be pregnant through the Holy Spirit. Because Joseph her husband was faithful to the law, and yet did not want to expose her to public disgrace, he had in mind to divorce her quietly.*

*But after he had considered this, an angel of the Lord appeared to him in a dream and said, 'Joseph son of David, do not be afraid to take Mary home as your wife, because what is conceived in her is from the Holy Spirit. She will give birth to a son, and you are to give him the name Jesus, because he will save his people from their sins.'* **(MATT. 1:18-21)**

Whoever says that people in those days did not understand the enormity of a virgin birth have obviously never listened to Joseph's views on the matter! He knew full well that something 'fishy' was going on when his wife-to-be was found to be pregnant. Knowing he was not the father, he made the only possible conclusion: Mary had been unfaithful to him. Given his strict allegiance to the law, he decided that it was not possible for him to go ahead with this marriage, but as a compassionate man he wanted to avoid all possible pain that might accrue to Mary as a result of the shame of her condition in those times.

All, so far, so normal. But then 'an angel of the Lord' appeared in a dream. Those who only read the birth narrative accounts of the Gospels are liable to think that angels appear around every corner in the Bible. In actual fact, they are highly rare. The rapidity of their appearances in these accounts shows that all heaven is on the move. ('Aslan is on the move!', as C.S. Lewis put it.) And it took an appearance of an angel to persuade Joseph that the facts of nature—that pregnant wife means that someone has made her pregnant, and if not him then, well…— were in this case being turned upside down.

We often give pride of place to Mary in these Christmas stories, on a human level, but spare a thought for Joseph. What faith must it have taken for him to accept the word not just of his wife, but even of the word of

God through the angel? Great faith. And this word from the angel to Joseph is of the origin of the virgin birth. This birth is 'from the Holy Spirit.' In a mystery beyond human understanding, and totally different from the crass ancient pagan myths of petty so-called gods sleeping with women, there is a veil drawn over the miraculous creation of this birth inside the womb of Mary. Joseph, not the human father, is given naming rights as if he were the father. Joseph will call the child 'Jesus'—or Savior—'because he will save his people from their sins' (verse 21). And He was already doing so. Bringing together a youthful marriage and setting it on a firm footing. Honoring the downcast, giving strength to a man by giving him a naming task, and the parental nurturing that it represented, to raise none other than the Son of God. Purpose for the purposeless, hope for the hopeless, salvation for sinners. Few of us like to think we need saving. Yet, in the deepest level of our humanity, we all do. Saving from pride. Saving from anxiety. Saving from hopelessness. Saving for something, too: in Joseph's case, to name the child whose name would be on the lips of all the peoples of the world, and before whose name one day every knee would bow.

*At the name of Jesus every knee shall bow,*
*every tongue confess Him King of glory now;*
*'tis the Father's pleasure we should call Him Lord,*
*who from the beginning was the mighty Word.*

*Humbled for a season, to receive a name
from the lips of sinners, unto whom He came;
faithfully He bore it spotless to the last,
brought it back victorious when from death He passed;
In your hearts enthrone Him; there let Him subdue
all that is not holy, all that is not true.
Look to Him, your Savior, in temptations' hour;
let His will enfold you in its light and power.*

**'At the Name of Jesus'** by Caroline M. Noel, 1870

# DIVINE JOY

*All this took place to fulfill what the Lord had said through the prophet: 'The virgin will conceive and give birth to a son, and they will call him Immanuel' (which means 'God with us'). When Joseph woke up, he did what the angel of the Lord had commanded him and took Mary home as his wife.* **(MATT. 1:22-24)**

One of the strangest apparent accidents of the text is that while Joseph has just been told by the angel to call the child 'Jesus,' we now learn that calling this child specifically 'Jesus' is actually in fulfillment of a promise to call Him 'Immanuel.' Such moments can cause head-scratching for the unaware reader: which is it, Jesus or Immanuel?

No doubt many answers have been given to this little conundrum, but the most likely, to my mind, is also the most helpful. 'Jesus' means 'God saves,' which is now underlining the true fulfillment of that name in the actual person of God Himself present (that is, 'Immanuel,' 'God with us') who is doing the saving.

It would be like calling someone 'William' and saying this is why he was called 'the conqueror.' For William is the name that was made famous by its designation to the ancient king 'William [or Wilhelm] the Conqueror,' and so to say that he is given this name in the same breath as saying that he is called 'the conqueror' only serves to confirm the true meaning of the name that he was given.

This is the most likely explanation, but it is also the most personally helpful. Not only is Matthew telling us that Jesus is fulfilling the great promise of Isaiah 7, he is also telling us how. He will be 'God with us' saving us—He is the King, and He is the saving King, too; He is God, and He is the Savior God, as well.

It is easy for us to swing from one extreme to the other in this regard. Cultures do, churches do, individuals do. One moment we make God so close to us that we cannot grasp His immensity. He is a friend, but little more than that. The next moment, though, we make Him so immense that the other idea of knowing Him, or of Him saving us, being with us, is as unfathomable as an elephant fitting in a telephone booth.

Instead, this tells us it is both. When we think of Jesus, we are to think of the great God of the whole universe.

And we are to think of this God as with us, present, for a specific purpose of saving. This combination, Matthew hints, does not denigrate His majesty, but exalts it as predicted long ago by Isaiah.

Would you then, this Christmas, fall at the feet of the God who is with us? Worship Him as above all, grander and greater than all, and yet at the same time also actually—by faith, real faith—your personal Savior? It is a strange combination, but like the mythical elixir of life, it is the melding of truth that changes the world. Immanuel, God with us.

> *Once in royal David's city,*
> *Stood a lowly cattle shed,*
> *Where a mother laid her Baby,*
> *In a manger for His bed:*
> *Mary was that mother mild,*
> *Jesus Christ, her little Child.*
>
> *He came down to earth from heaven,*
> *Who is God and Lord of all,*
> *And His shelter was a stable,*
> *And His cradle was a stall:*
> *With the poor, and mean, and lowly,*
> *Lived on earth our Savior holy.*

**'Once in David's Royal City'** by Cecil F. Alexander, 1848

"

GOD DOES NOT COME
TO US WITH FORCE
TO OVERWHELM
OUR RESISTANCE, A
BLITZKRIEG OF WAR TO
DESTROY US. HE COMES
TO US IN HUMILITY.

(p.37)

## DECEMBER 9:

# SILENT JOY

*In those days Caesar Augustus issued a decree that a census should be taken of the entire Roman world. (This was the first census that took place while Quirinius was governor of Syria.) And everyone went to their own town to register.*

*So Joseph also went up from the town of Nazareth in Galilee to Judea, to Bethlehem the town of David, because he belonged to the house and line of David. He went there to register with Mary, who was pledged to be married to him and was expecting a child. While they were there, the time came for the baby to be born, and she gave birth to her firstborn, a son. She wrapped him in cloths and placed him in a manger, because there was no guest room available for them.* **(LUKE 2:1-7)**

This is a scene that has been played out in innumerable Christmas pageants—but what does it mean? There is Mary and there is Joseph, and there is the 'inn' in which there is no room for them. It's a story that resonates with significance this Christmas for refugees, for the homeless, for those struggling to make ends meet, and for every mother that ever was. There's a mad dash to Bethlehem to fulfill the dictate of a distant emperor, studiously recorded by Luke to ensure that future generations would know this happened and when it occurred, too.

Scholars have established the veracity of these events (which you can follow up in classic commentaries like that by I. Howard Marshall's, *The Gospel of Luke*), and Luke is as good a historian here as he is elsewhere. They go, they arrive, they have nowhere to stay. And Mary—the virgin Mary as the Gospel accounts have already established—gives birth to Jesus, the child who is so named by Joseph on the instruction of the angel to make it clear that this child is the Savior and is also the divine God with us, Immanuel. He is 'God Saves.'

But what does it mean? What does it mean for us this Christmas? Is it only a sentimental story that resonates with Christmas cheer around smoking log fires and Christmas lights festooning a Christmas tree? Is it merely a description of an event that truly took place, a factual record that we can acknowledge as true and keep on going on our merry way this Christmas? Or is there a message, designed by Luke, inspired by the Author, that is intended to give us joy this Christmas?

There is a phrase now in common usage which relates to the message and meaning of this passage for us this Christmas. The phrase is 'under the radar.' The picture is of someone having a radar screen, scanning for incoming threats or opportunities, and something manages to get all the way past this by flying 'under the radar,' going unnoticed. Recently a new American destroyer was released that has a different ability; this 'stealth' ship appears only as a small shipping vessel on radar screens.

The message of this extraordinary account is how God gets under our radar. We hold up barriers, protective defense mechanisms, designed to protect us from the vulnerability of realizing that we are really and truly loved. God does not come to us with force to overwhelm our resistance, a blitzkrieg of war to destroy us. He comes to us in humility. He is, in the brilliant words of the famous Christmas carol, 'silently pleading.' Under our radar of pride, under our radar of insecurity, under our radar of fear that if we 'let Him in' He will (like so many others have) also 'let us down.'

And God comes as a baby. Soft enough, vulnerable enough, to soften the hardest hearts, and open up the toughest shells, and get beneath the most vigilant radar watchers trying to keep out divine love.

*What child is this, who, laid to rest,*
*On Mary's lap is sleeping?*

*...This, this is Christ the King,*
*Whom shepherds guard and angels sing:*

*...Why lies He in such mean estate,*
*Where ox and donkeys are feeding?*

*Good Christians, fear, for sinners here*
*The silent Word is pleading.*

*Nails, spears shall pierce Him through,*
*the cross He bore for me, for you.*

*Hail, hail the Word made flesh,*
*the Babe, the Son of Mary.*

**'What Child Is This?'** by William Chatterton Dix, 1865

# TRUE JOY

*And there were shepherds living out in the fields nearby, keeping watch over their flocks at night. An angel of the Lord appeared to them, and the glory of the Lord shone around them, and they were terrified. But the angel said to them, 'Do not be afraid. I bring you good news that will cause great joy for all the people. Today in the town of David a Savior has been born to you; he is the Messiah, the Lord. This will be a sign to you: You will find a baby wrapped in cloths and lying in a manger.'* **(LUKE 2:8-12)**

This text is made famous nowadays for being the passage that Linus quotes at the end of the endearing little *Peanuts* movie about Christmas. He is finally asked, after much exasperation from Charlie Brown, to tell everyone the real meaning of Christmas. 'I'll tell you, Charlie Brown.' Linus steps up to the microphone, the lights in the house dim, the spotlight is on Linus, and he recites this passage from Luke's Gospel. This is the real meaning of Christmas.

What does it mean for us this Christmas? Here are four lessons about the meaning of Christmas this year derived from what I will call affectionately the 'Linus Christmas passage':

1. **It's not about the commercialization of gifts and presents and 'things.'** Most people reading this post will recognize this point as something of a tired 'trope' recited ad nauseam by preachers at Christmastime. But the reason why it is such a common warning is because it is such a common trap. Everyone enjoys receiving something nice for Christmas. Everyone is happy—at least for a moment—when they open a present under the tree and it is exactly what they wanted. On the other hand, as you grow older, such moments are less frequent, and even when you are young they are short-lived. Who among us can honestly remember what we received for Christmas even last year? No, the real 'magic' of Christmas is something far more than what you can buy in a store.

2. **It's not about social feelings of goodwill to one another.** This is a less common warning sounded from the pulpit because it can come across as

being 'Scrooge-like,' but Christmas is not simply about goodwill and cheer to all people around us. It is a good thing to be kind at Christmas, and that 'Christmas spirit' is certainly worth maintaining and doing so far beyond the mere confines of Advent. But the message of Christmas is emptied of any real meaning if it is merely about being kind. Why be kind at Christmas instead of at any other time of the year? Why make a special effort at Christmas to celebrate Christmas if the celebration is merely about being generous to each other? Christmas will 'run out of steam' as a celebration unless it has some distinct meaning far beyond a winter solstice respite from the cold, or a tradition passed down from generation to generation. Traditions, when good, are good things, but they too will disappear unless we know the 'why,' a reason for them.

3. **It is good news!** That is, Christmas is essentially a message, a message about Someone, a message that is intrinsically, and overwhelmingly, positive and encouraging and enlightening and uplifting. This is why we are spending time looking at the Christmas story during these devotionals. There is a *message* to Christmas. Christmas is not only an experience, it has cognitive content; it has meaning because it has a message. What is that message? Essentially it is a message about the breaking

into this world of a divine Savior in the person of a human baby. That message is so extraordinary, certainly supernatural, so mind-blowing, that when encapsulated, when verbalized, when expressed, when depicted, it has unerring power to move beyond human limitations and cause the hardest hearted to melt in tears before the baby of Bethlehem.

4. **It causes great joy!** That is, Christmas has something about it that can lighten the darkness of the most traumatized, as well as further give reason for rejoicing to those who are more temperate or whose circumstances are less challenging. It is well-known in the caring professions that the 'holidays,' the Christmas season, is the worst season of the year for marital conflict, family meltdowns, depressive events, and the like. There are at least two reasons for this. One, during the Christmas season people spend a lot more time with each other. Increased interaction either highlights the positive value of those relationships or forces into close proximity those who are barely on speaking terms. Two, the expectations of Christmas as a materialistic, experiential event are so elevated in our culture that anything that does not live up to these unattainable goals is a letdown. If at any other time of the year we had one tenth of the experience of most of our Christmases, we would

be ecstatic. But do they live up to the joy of the ending of *It's a Wonderful Life*? By the same token, people we love who are not with us are doubly missed at Christmas. The cure for such Christmas letdowns, for whatever reason, is to understand the real nature of the joy of Christmas—which is, as Linus and Luke would both say, 'a baby wrapped in cloths and lying in a manger.' Focus on Him, the Christ King born in poverty for your salvation, and joy will follow.

*While shepherds watched*
*Their flocks by night*
*All seated on the ground*
*The angel of the Lord came down*
*And glory shone around,*

*'Fear not,' said he,*
*For mighty dread*
*Had seized their troubled minds*
*'Glad tidings of great joy I bring*
*To you and all mankind.'*

*'To you in David's*
*Town this day*
*Is born of David's line*
*The Savior who is Christ the Lord*
*And this shall be the sign.'*

*'The heavenly Babe*
*You there shall find*
*To human view displayed*
*And meanly wrapped*
*In swathing bands*
*And in a manger laid.'*

**'While Shepherds Watched Their Flocks'** by Nahum Tate, 1703

# PEACEFUL JOY

*Suddenly a great company of the heavenly host appeared with the angel, praising God and saying, 'Glory to God in the highest heaven, and on earth peace to those on whom his favor rests.'* **(LUKE 2:13-14)**

The word 'suddenly' introduces a moment that must have stuck in the minds of these shepherds ever after! They were 'suddenly' surrounded by a huge crowd, suggesting not just a few but a massive assembly, and with a touch of the military band to it. The army of heaven had turned up, the marching band, loud, moving, triumphant, impressive, unmissable.

Such glorious beings as these heavenly warriors would naturally and rightly accord attention to themselves, but without a moment's hesitation, they strike up a praise song that centers not on themselves, and certainly not on us, but on God. 'Glory to God,' and not just any kind of glory but the 'highest' kind of praise and adulation that could be considered.

But while this praise is God-centered, that does not mean that our needs are unconsidered. In fact, the very idea that something could be glorious to God but uncaring about people is a contradiction in terms. The true God and His true glory expand forever in love. His bountiful care and compassion and power overflow with attention towards us. In the divinest of ironies, the more we glorify God, the more 'peace' we will find on earth.

That 'peace on earth' is so needed today. How will it come about? Only as we proclaim the glory of God as revealed in Jesus Christ. The hope for peace on earth is not (finally) world summits or international peace conferences. It is not endlessly churning committee meetings in innumerable ecumenical dialogue. It is not the power of one nation to dominate another. There is a reason why the authorities and governments 'bear the sword,' to bring about justice and order, and for their hard task we are commanded to pray that God would give them wisdom and strength. But that order can only at best be external, like the order of building a wall between warring parties or separating sparring fighters for a moment under the rules of the boxing ring. To have real 'peace on earth' requires something more, something transcendent, something that affects us internally.

Real peace may only derive from the 'favor of God,' His grace and mercy. It is according to God's gracious will, His good pleasure, His sovereign action and intervention.

This Christmas, then, would you seek 'peace on earth' by praying for those in authority that they would act with justice, compassion, and wise holy strength? Would you seek 'peace on earth' by (re)centering your life upon the glory of God, ordering your world and family and individual trajectory around honoring the One above whom none (not even us) is to be honored? And would you seek 'peace on earth' by proclaiming the gospel of God's grace, favor, and good pleasure, so that those around us can hear of Christ and His peace this Christmas?

> *Jesus this song you wrote*
> *The words are sticking in my throat*
> *Peace on Earth*
> *Hear it every Christmas time*
> *But hope and history won't rhyme*
> *So what's it worth?*
> *This peace on Earth*

**'Peace on Earth'** by U2, 1998

> *I heard the bells on Christmas Day*
> *Their old, familiar carols play,*
> *and wild and sweet*

*The words repeat*
*Of peace on earth, good-will to men!*

*...*

*And in despair I bowed my head;*
*'There is no peace on earth,' I said;*
*'For hate is strong,*
*And mocks the song*
*Of peace on earth, good-will to men!'*
*Then pealed the bells more loud and deep:*
*'God is not dead, nor doth He sleep;*
*The Wrong shall fail,*
*The Right prevail,*
*With peace on earth, good-will to men.'*

**'I Heard the Bells on Christmas Day'**
by Henry Wadsworth Longfellow, Christmas Day 1863

# LOUD JOY

*When the angels had left them and gone into heaven, the shepherds said to one another, 'Let's go to Bethlehem and see this thing that has happened, which the Lord has told us about.'*

*So they hurried off and found Mary and Joseph, and the baby, who was lying in the manger. When they had seen him, they spread the word concerning what had been told them about this child, and all who heard it were amazed at what the shepherds said to them. But Mary treasured up all these things and pondered them in her heart. The shepherds returned, glorifying and praising God for all the things they had heard and seen, which were just as they had been told.* **(LUKE 2:15-20)**

The shepherds, being practical men of action, decided immediately to go and discover whether what they had been told was true. Luke does not tell us exactly how they found Mary and Joseph, but after 'apparently' little difficulty (how many babies were being born in a cattle shed in any particular town at any particular moment?), they find things to be precisely as they had been told.

Their response, Luke tells us, is after they have 'seen him' they go out and 'spread the word' concerning Him, or more particularly 'what had been told them about this child.' The message they spread is not just a 'nativity' scene, but the extraordinary message that the angels had given them about this newborn King. As the shepherds—the ancient equivalent of cowboys, not the precious puny figures of some pageants—tell everyone they can find about Jesus, their word has a suitably dramatic effect. The people are 'amazed,' astounded, their minds are blown at the idea that God is on the move, and His vehicle for intervention is a baby born in a manger.

Mary's response is quieter. Why? Why was she not raucously excited as well? Apart from the physical demands of birth which would have kept her from too much physical exertion immediately afterwards, Mary is 'treasuring' these things. Like a typical mother in some ways, she is recording in her mind and heart every first moment of her own beautiful baby boy. But she is also 'pondering' them, for she is far from a typical first-time mother, and she has much to chew over in her mind if she is to figure out what it will mean to bring up baby Jesus! Finally, the shepherds return, praising God. Everything was just as they had been told.

The shepherds' loud joy is a rebuke to us timorous souls who find it hard to quietly invite, even by email or text message, anyone else to come and hear about Christ at Christmas. If they, so new to everything about Christ, could be so excited, and so unselfconscious in 'spreading the word,' could we not find one person to tell about Jesus this Christmas? One person to invite to hear the gospel preached this Christmas?

But if the shepherds are a rebuke to our temerity, Mary is a rebuke to our superficiality. She thinks things over, she understands deeply, she does not let this first Christmas rush over her in a haste of activity and busyness. If Mary, who had much to do, and many problems to fix, could take the time to 'ponder' these things in her heart, could we not find time this Christmas to read the Christmas story, become involved in church, take the time to reorient our souls around the real meaning of Christmas—the Christ-child born King!

> *Joy to the world! the Savior reigns*
> *Let men their songs employ*
> *While fields and floods*

*Rocks, hills and plains*
*Repeat the sounding joy*
*Repeat the sounding joy*
*Repeat, repeat the sounding joy.*

**'Joy to the World'** by Isaac Watts, 1719

# OBEDIENT JOY

*On the eighth day, when it was time to circumcise the child, he was named Jesus, the name the angel had given him before he was conceived.*

*When the time came for the purification rites required by the Law of Moses, Joseph and Mary took him to Jerusalem to present him to the Lord (as it is written in the Law of the Lord, 'Every firstborn male is to be consecrated to the Lord'), and to offer a sacrifice in keeping with what is said in the Law of the Lord: 'a pair of doves or two young pigeons.'* **(LUKE 2:21-24)**

Mary and Joseph proceed to do what parents of their religious convictions at their time did. Jesus is circumcised in the normal way. And then He is taken to the temple, according to the 'Law of the Lord.' It is often said that the sacrifice chosen ('a pair of doves or two young pigeons') indicates that they were poor.

What is interesting about all of this from our point of view is how careful Mary and Joseph are to obey the Law. There is no sense that their family were 'radicals' or that Jesus was being set up to challenge the institution in the sense of overturn the prevailing Word of God. No, as Jesus Himself would frequently insist, He had not come to abolish the Law but to fulfill it. Jesus was the right understanding of the Law in His own person, and now He (and His family) was living life in every way to fulfill all the requirements of the Law so that He could be the perfectly righteous person, live the perfectly righteous life, and die the perfectly righteous death, for unrighteous people like you and me.

We can take comfort, then, from the fact that Jesus fulfilled the Law. He lived the perfect life and died the perfect death so that imperfect people might, through faith in Him, be declared righteous before God because of Him and His own perfect life. What a comfort this is at Christmas! Christmas, with all its expectations of a 'perfect' house, and a 'perfect' family, and a 'perfect' present or gift, a 'perfect' Christmas tree. And in the perfections of Christ, our imperfections are covered, and we can be free to be who we truly are. Not, of course, that we should not strive to improve and do better in life. However imperfect finally our achievements may be, we still must aim to do all we can for Christ and His kingdom. But because of Christ's 'perfections,' we can serve in freedom—without guilt, with joy, and with great peace.

It also reminds us of the need for us all to obey God's Law. Sometimes its prescriptions may not make sense to us. We might wish that God had said something different or required something easier than a 'trip to the temple,' or a membership of a church, or a faithfulness to a troublesome relationship at home. But, in humility, recognizing the humility of Christ and of Christ's family in this instance, we too can humble ourselves under God so that in due time He will lift us up. We submit to one another out of reverence of Christ. We do the right thing, according to what God tells us in His Word, because Christ Himself submitted to the Law, and we do it with joyful confidence because Christ's joyful faithfulness covers our own unrighteous failures.

Sometimes such obedience feels like a 'sacrifice' too. But it is a sacrifice that leads to Christmas joy!

*Good Christian friends, rejoice*
*With heart and soul and voice*
*Now ye need not fear the grave:*
*Peace! Peace!*

*Jesus Christ was born to save*
*Calls you one and calls you all*
*To gain His everlasting hall*
*Christ was born to save*
*Christ was born to save.*

# MATURE JOY

*Now there was a man in Jerusalem called Simeon, who was righteous and devout. He was waiting for the consolation of Israel, and the Holy Spirit was on him. It had been revealed to him by the Holy Spirit that he would not die before he had seen the Lord's Messiah. Moved by the Spirit, he went into the temple courts. When the parents brought in the child Jesus to do for him what the custom of the Law required, Simeon took him in his arms and praised God, saying:*

*'Sovereign Lord, as you have promised,*
    *you may now dismiss your servant in peace.*
*For my eyes have seen your salvation,*
    *which you have prepared in the sight of all nations:*
*a light for revelation to the Gentiles,*
    *and the glory of your people Israel.'* **(LUKE 2:25-32)**

Speaking personally, Simeon is one of my favorite characters in these early nativity stories! I can see him now, hoary headed, white haired, shuffling faithfully in the temple courts, filled with the Holy Spirit to the last drop of his personality. I have known men like him, old (we assume Simeon was aged because the text tells us he had been waiting, we assume for a long time, and that after seeing Jesus he is ready to die), yet while old, also renewed day by day with the power of the Holy Spirit. There is an evident godliness to such men and women. It is not fanciful to suggest that it would be obvious that Simeon was one of those godly people who everyone knew the 'Holy Spirit was on him.' They carry an air to them, a presence, and to be with them immediately raises your own game spiritually, in the same way that when Michael Jordan walks on the basketball court you'd better do your very best.

And so 'moved by the Spirit'—by what operation Luke, often in his Gospel emphasizing the work of the Spirit, does not tell us—Simeon goes into the temple courts. Something in him harmonized with the presence of the Christ, and immediately he took Him in his arms and praised God! What an extraordinary thing it must have been to be the parents of such a child. When you go to church the most eminently godly man, respected above all others, rushes over as fast as his wobbly legs will carry him, asks to hold the child, and loudly and spontaneously, in front of everyone, praises God for your child! That was an event to remember, and record as Luke does for us his readers.

Simeon's words are deep with meaning. Jesus is the Messiah, that much is plain. Everything now is at peace with Simeon, for he has seen the Messiah with his own shadowy aged eyes. But what does it mean to be the Messiah? Simeon tells us. He is 'salvation,' and not salvation only for Israel, but for 'all nations': 'a light for revelation to the Gentiles, and the glory of your people Israel.' What could be better than to have been present at such moment when the glory of Israel was revealed to Simeon, the saintliest man for generations, filled with the Spirit, prophetically uttering the call of God to all nations through Jesus the Messiah King?

Luke tells us this story as another way of showing us that the godly of Israel recognized the person of Jesus. It was not just the shepherds, not just the angels, but the godliest elder saint that anyone could ever imagine. This Christmas, then, would you, as another year passes by, and whether you are young or old, make a fresh resolution to ensure that more maturity, and greater years, means increased devotion to the Christ King?

Sometimes we think that devotion, enthusiasm, energy, spontaneity, emotion for God is something that is okay when you are young, but as you get older should be replaced by more detached commitment. Let Simeon show you otherwise this Christmas. Let his example, this man on whom was the Holy Spirit, and who embraced the baby Jesus with evident passion, as well as reason and scriptural insight, lead us all, young and old, to grow up by growing into more and more praise of the 'glory of Israel'!

*Lord, now lettest thou thy servant depart in peace according to thy word.*
*For mine eyes have seen thy salvation,*
*Which thou hast prepared before the face of all people;*
*To be a light to lighten the Gentiles and to be the glory of thy people Israel.*

Book of Common Prayer, 1662

# DECISIVE JOY

*The child's father and mother marveled at what was said about him. Then Simeon blessed them and said to Mary, his mother: 'This child is destined to cause the falling and rising of many in Israel, and to be a sign that will be spoken against, so that the thoughts of many hearts will be revealed. And a sword will pierce your own soul too.'* (LUKE 2:33-35)

The astonishing words of Simeon (Luke 2:30-32), calling Jesus 'salvation' and the 'light' for the nations and the 'glory' of Israel, understandably left Joseph and Mary blown away. What on earth was this godly old man talking about? How could he be describing their little infant in such grandiose, nearly sacrilegious, terms? What could it all mean?

Godly to the end, Simeon responds not by trying to squeeze more theology down the throats of Joseph and Mary than they were at this stage able to swallow, but instead he responds by ministering to them. He 'blessed' them, pronouncing that what he has said, far beyond their ability to understand in any sense at this point, would nonetheless be good. It came with a blessing, and Simeon underscored that for them by, in some way, formally blessing them when he observed they were disturbed by the scale of his predictions about the career of their baby Jesus.

But then having blessed them and assured them of the good intentions of God and the blessing that this child is to them, he does not let them mistake his meaning. Jesus is going to be a divisive figure. It is good if you are for Him, bad if you are against Him. He will cause the 'falling and rising of many in Israel.' There will be a changing of the guard. Things are going to turn upside down, and Jesus, the ultimate change agent, is going to be at the tip of the spear of God's movement.

Given that this is what is going to happen, almost inevitably Jesus will have enemies. He will be a 'sign that will be spoken against.' People will speak against Him and campaign against Him. And in so doing, in taking a stance against Jesus, their own hearts will be revealed. Nothing says that you are against God, really and truly, like coming out against God's anointed. Those who had hidden behind comfortable expressions of traditional piety in the degenerate form of religiosity taking place at the time in Israel would find that they could not agree with the purifying fire of Christ, and when they opposed Christ, what would be shown is who they really are. If you say you are for God, but then God Himself turns up and you are actually against God in the person of Jesus Christ the Son of God, then apparently you were never for God at all.

Even today the same dynamic takes place. People are quite often vaguely in favor of 'god' or 'the divine' or 'spirituality.' They may be in favor of a 'god' of this religion or that. But when you speak of Jesus—well, then it shows what people really think about God, because Jesus is really God.

Simeon is even compassionate, and pastorally wise enough, to tell Mary the real deal in terms of the impact on her own life. To be the mother of such a man, the God-Man Christ, a man who would have such an impact, and be so persecuted, and even crucified, would not be easy. In fact, 'a sword will pierce your own soul too.'

One of the great risks, even dangers, of Christmas, you see, is that we domesticate it. Christ as a baby is so cute, so cuddly, so inoffensive, so easy to accept. But this baby will grow. And one day He will return. What you make of the man who threw the money changers out of the temple, who cast demons out of the demoniac, who rejected the hypocritical Pharisee, and ate with sinners and tax collectors, what you think of Him will one day be finally revealed when He returns. Would you, then, this Christmas be one of those who 'rise' because of Jesus? To do that, you need first bow before Jesus.

*And our eyes at last shall see Him,*
*Through His own redeeming love;*
*For that Child so dear and gentle,*
*Is our Lord in heaven above:*
*And He leads His children on,*
*To the place where He is gone.*

**'Once in Royal David's City'** by Cecil Frances Alexander, 1848

# IMMEDIATE JOY

*There was also a prophet, Anna, the daughter of Penuel, of the tribe of Asher. She was very old; she had lived with her husband seven years after her marriage, and then was a widow until she was eighty-four. She never left the temple but worshiped night and day, fasting and praying. Coming up to them at that very moment, she gave thanks to God and spoke about the child to all who were looking forward to the redemption of Jerusalem.* (LUKE 2:36-38)

As if the drama of the moment, Jesus' first visit to the temple, had not yet been sufficiently heightened by the extraordinary announcement of the godly Simeon, now there is another shining encounter. Anna, a prophet who is very old and has been widowed for many years (we assume), having only been married for seven years before her husband died, now eighty-four years old, an advanced aged by any culture's reckoning, also comes to see the family.

She was always in the temple, giving herself over to worship, all the time, fasting and praying. Anna was one of the great godly, devoted examples of piety that adorned the temple in those days. 'At that very moment,' while the words of Simeon were still ringing in their ears and the ears of everyone else who would have heard them, Anna comes up to them too and publicly 'gave thanks to God.' She praises God for this extraordinary, supernatural child, moved to adulation and worship at that very moment in sheer joy at the sight of the Christ-child.

She also 'spoke about the child.' She begins a mini-lecture or instruction, using the child as the perfect visual aid, to explain the real hope for Jerusalem, the 'redemption of Jerusalem,' to all those who were hoping for a restoration of the glory days, and the coming of the Messiah. She praises God, and she speaks of what this child means for the plan of God to redeem His people.

Once again, we cannot help but wonder at the mental state of Mary or Joseph at this 'moment,' spoken to by Simeon, and now by Anna, when they had turned up at the temple to do their religious duty by their firstborn. They must have been excited, terrified, surprised, scared, rejoicing, praising—all at once! But the account passes over the reactions of Mary and Joseph in this place with little notice. All attention is on Simeon, and now on Anna, and what they are doing and what it means. We are meant to be caught up in the response of Simeon and Anna. We are meant to see this child in our temple courts, and like Anna 'at that very moment' give praise to God and speak of what this child means for the redemption of all who believe.

Would you, this Christmas, respond like Anna with praise and proclamation? Would you consciously, deliberately, right now, praise God for Jesus and the birth of the Christ-child for His people's redemption? Perhaps sing a much-beloved carol ('O Holy Night,' for instance).

Take a moment now, this very moment, to praise God for Jesus. And with that praise on your lips, look around at those who are longing for redemption—for their country, their church, their family—and speak of how it is that the gospel of Jesus can be the hope for all nations and the redemption of all who believe.

*O Holy Night! The stars are brightly shining,*
*It is the night of the dear Savior's birth.*
*Long lay the world in sin and error pining.*
*Till He appeared and the Spirit felt its worth.*
*A thrill of hope the weary world rejoices,*
*For yonder breaks a new and glorious morn.*

*Fall on your knees! Oh, hear the angel voices!*
*O night divine, the night when Christ was born;*
*O night, O Holy Night, O night divine!*
*O night, O Holy Night, O night divine!*

**'O Holy Night'** by Placide Cappeau,
set to music by Adolphe Adam, 1847

# WISE JOY

*After Jesus was born in Bethlehem in Judea, during the time of King Herod, Magi from the east came to Jerusalem and asked, 'Where is the one who has been born king of the Jews? We saw his star when it rose and have come to worship him.'* (MATTHEW 2:1-2)

The visit of the Magi, or the wise men, or the kings from the Orient, is one of the most well-known, best loved, and at the same time least understood portions of the famous Christmas story. Who were the Magi? What does their arrival signify? Why is it included in the Christmas narrative? What are we meant to learn from their visit to discover Jesus? What was this 'star' that they followed?

Many different theories down through the years have been proposed regarding the nature of this star, and neither time nor space allow us now to survey them all and give an accurate, judicious assessment of their veracity. In brief, some have wondered whether it was some kind of shooting star, others whether it was some sort of well-known stellar event of various possibilities. Others have simply said that it was supernatural.

We do, at least, have the time to be sure we do not misplace, or inadvertently confuse, the 'supernatural.' Clearly, the birth of Jesus was supernatural by any orthodox biblical understanding, and so whether or not we think that God directly 'moved' a star to lead the wise men, or whether He employed some other more 'natural' event to accomplish the same end, the whole thing is nonetheless God-ordained, supernatural, and we who believe in the virgin birth need not balk at a moving star. There is no point in swallowing the camel of the incarnation to choke on the gnat of a star. If God is God, then He can do as He will.

Normally, miracles do not occur. They are rare by definition; otherwise, they would not be called 'miracles.' But we cannot rule them out of the possible and still maintain belief in a God of miracles as well. It is also quite possible that these 'Magi,' the wise men, schooled in the ancient, learned habit of watching the stars, would have interpreted a historic constellation as meaning a king, and a king of the Jews, and then have traveled to discover the meaning of this 'sign,' in that sense 'following the star.'

At any rate, they are here. But why? What is the point of their arrival? They are an immediate, obvious, and clear message that this Jesus is King, not only of the Jews, but King of the world, the universe, and 'the east' as well. People are traveling from 'afar' to worship Him. Whether or not they fully understand the meaning of the One whom they worship (how could they fully understand, how can we fully understand?), is in one sense beside the point. They are there, symbolic of the universal reach of this particular King at this particular moment. They are paying Him homage, are drawn by His majesty, and bow at His presence. This King is King of the Magi too. He is King of the learned as well as the simple, of the west as well as the east, of the king as well as the shepherd, of the star gazer as well as the book reader.

It is always surprising who Jesus calls to Himself. Genetics do not tell the whole story, nor does family upbringing. At Christmas there are Magi too. Perhaps that is you, or someone you know. Perhaps you feel like you are about as much a part of things, have about as much a sense of belonging, as Magi at the original Christmas in Bethlehem. This King can be your King too. He is not just for those who are already 'in the club.' You may not understand everything yet, but if you come to worship the Christ, then at Christmas you have come to the right person and the right place.

*O Star of wonder, star of night*
*Star with royal beauty bright*
*Westward leading, still proceeding*
*Guide us to thy Perfect Light*

**'We Three Kings'** by John Henry Hopkins, 1857

**DECEMBER 18:**

# DISTURBING JOY

*When King Herod heard this he was disturbed, and all Jerusalem with him. When he had called together all the people's chief priests and teachers of the law, he asked them where the Messiah was to be born. 'In Bethlehem in Judea,' they replied, 'for this is what the prophet has written:*

*"But you, Bethlehem, in the land of Judah,*
  *are by no means least among the rulers of Judah;*
*for out of you will come a ruler*
  *who will shepherd my people Israel."'*
**(MATTHEW 2:3-6)**

Naturally enough, Herod is disturbed. As a controversial leader in his own time—questionable heritage, unedifyingly close relationship with the Roman powers that be, morally suspect—to be told that specially

73

designated foreign ambassadors have come looking for the one who has been born king of your kingdom would inevitably be disturbing. It would be like a president of a dictatorship being told that some foreign dignitaries had come inquiring about who was going to be the next dictator in your place. You would feel threatened if you were that dictator, or in this case if you were this Herod king.

But it is not only the king, it is also 'all Jerusalem with him.' There is a sense in which any potential political upheaval is likely to be damaging, at least initially, and would cause those who like life to stay the same to be also in some ways too 'disturbed.' When you are not sure what is happening, and you know that whatever happens will have big consequences for your life, then you are likely also to be 'disturbed' by news related to such a change of power coming down the road.

Herod is savvy enough to proceed carefully. He knows that in his time the 'king' and the 'Messiah' were synonymous in prophetic thought, as 'Messiah' means anointed one, and the king was the anointed one. He calls the religious authorities together and asks them to tell him where it is thought that the new Messiah King will be born. (It is interesting to note that the king himself did not know how to answer this question about the Messiah but needed special religious instruction to find the meaning in the Scriptures, given that kings of the Jews were meant to be well schooled in the Scriptures.) The religious authorities give him the standard answer, and in so doing, they reveal the common expectation, as well as the biblical prophecy from Micah, about this coming King Messiah.

He will be a ruler, He will come from Bethlehem, He will shepherd His people. Perhaps they judiciously, given their perilous position before this Herod king, leave out some aspects of the quotation that might be particularly offensive. 'He shall stand and shepherd his flock in the strength of the LORD, in the majesty of the name of the LORD his God. And they shall dwell secure, for now he shall be great to the ends of the earth. And he shall be their peace.' (Micah 5-4, ESV). Those words of greatness and fame and peace because of just rule might well have been too much for an intemperate Herod to handle. They also, perhaps not because of Herod, perhaps because of their own bias, leave out another aspect of the quotation, one that hints of the Messiah King's divine origin: 'whose origin is from of old, from ancient days' (Micah 5:2).

At any rate, this Messiah King brings a disturbance—and in some way or other to all. He is our peace. But first we must have our tendency to want to be kings of our own domain 'disturbed.' Only when we bow before Him this Christmas can we find that He will shepherd us with strength and be our peace.

*O little town of Bethlehem*
*How still we see thee lie*
*Above thy deep and dreamless sleep*
*The silent stars go by.*
*Yet in thy dark streets shineth*
*The everlasting Light;*
*The hopes and fears of all the years*
*Are met in thee tonight.*

**'O Little Town of Bethlehem'** by Phillips Brooks, 1868

# TRUE JOY

*Then Herod called the Magi secretly and found out from them the exact time the star had appeared. He sent them to Bethlehem and said, 'Go and search carefully for the child. As soon as you find him, report to me, so that I too may go and worship him.'* **(MATTHEW 2:7-8)**

In the Bible, Herod comes across as a real piece of work. Likewise, the historical accounts of his behavior are not favorable to his reputation—redeemable as we all are by grace if God wills. Herod acts with suitable cunning that fits his malevolent reputation. He calls the Magi 'secretly'—anything done in secret, in the dark, has a reason not to want to be in the light. There may well be, and of course are in certain circumstances, reasons to keep confidences, but secret political deals in smoke-filled rooms are rarely commendable. This one was certainly not commendable. He wants to know more details.

Perhaps his reason for bringing the Magi back to him, and for them actually returning to him willingly, was to feign an academic interest in the astrological stargazing technicalities that so clearly fascinated these 'wise men from the east.' Having gotten them back into his presence and won them over with pleasing academic discussions about their passion, he comes to the real point at hand. He 'sent them to Bethlehem.' He wants to know where the child is, and what could be a better way of discovering that than using these inadvertent and unwitting Magi as tools for that end.

The Magi themselves had innocent, noble, and high reasons to find the child, and so their 'searching carefully' for the child would not rouse suspicions among friends and neighbors the same way that a cohort of Herod's guards or some secret police or agent would arouse suspicion. The child and His parents are less likely to hide from Herod if they do not know that Herod is looking for them. If Stalin's agents came knocking around the neighborhood asking where a certain person was, then people would likely be suspicious. If a friendly foreigner, with no apparent agenda, asks to find a local newborn child, then the good-willed friends and neighbors are far more likely to be forthcoming about where the child might be.

Apparently, Herod is not above outright lying. He wants to go to Bethlehem too and 'worship him.' Who was he kidding? He was pretending to be an outright seeker after God, a pious devotee, someone who wanted nothing better than to bow the knee before the Christ-child. Unfortunately, there are those who pretend to be interested in spiritual things for no other reason than for what they can get out of those spiritual things.

When religion is popular, some will join and 'worship' in order to make good contacts for their business or their career. Their real agenda is quite different than the worship songs or the preaching or the service events of the worshiping church. They are really there for something else—to make contacts with people for their own ends—and come across as a good person by being seen to go to 'worship.'

When religion is not popular, then people may want to 'worship' for other reasons: to find out where the worship center is, secretly hidden, to hear what is being said by the preacher so it can be maliciously reported to the news, to undermine from within by lies and gossip. Unfortunately, not all that glitters is gold, and it is wise for churches to not only welcome all to come to worship Jesus, but to have some sort of membership process to establish, in the judgment of charity, who is really a member of Christ.

This part of the Christmas story reminds us that while there is much about Christmas that is kindly sentimental, sweet, and deliciously peaceful, even at the first Christmas, Christ came to a world desperately in need of peace. If this Christ-child can rule at the first Bethlehem, and in that place with the Roman Empire and Herod as king, then He can certainly rule in our world today and bring peace to us all through genuine worship of Him.

*How silently, how silently*
*The wondrous gift is given!*
*So God imparts to human hearts*
*The blessings of His heaven.*
*No ear may hear His coming,*
*But in this world of sin,*
*Where meek souls will receive Him still,*
*The dear Christ enters in.*

**'O Little Town of Bethlehem'** by Phillips Brooks, 1868

## DECEMBER 20:

# WORSHIPFUL JOY

*After they had heard the king, they went on their way,*
*and the star they had seen when it rose went ahead of*
*them until it stopped over the place where the child*
*was. When they saw the star, they were overjoyed.*
*On coming to the house, they saw the child with his*
*mother Mary, and they bowed down and worshiped*
*him. Then they opened their treasures and presented*
*him with gifts of gold, frankincense and myrrh. And*
*having been warned in a dream not to go back to*
*Herod, they returned to their country by another*
*route.* **(MATTHEW 2:9-12)**

The Magi, apparently none the wiser to Herod's nefarious
scheming yet, 'went on their way,' and followed the star
to 'the place where the child was.' God, in His sovereign
power, uses this 'star' to guide them to the location of
the divine Son of God. 'They were overjoyed'—really,

truly joyful— 'when they saw the star,' realizing that their journey had come to an end and that they had discovered that which they had sought.

They go in to the 'house,' they see the child and the child's mother Mary, and they do what none could have predicted. They 'bowed down,' bending low as a sign of obeisance. Had they treated King Herod this way? We are not told so. The account emphasizes the fact that the king they truly recognized was this child King, and they fall before Him and give Him kingly honor.

But not only do they give Him kingly honor, they also accord Him worship: they 'worshiped him.' Whether or not the Magi can be said to have understood all the intricacies of Christology that, for instance, Paul writes about in Colossians, we can see in all accuracy that in this child it was all there for them to see. The majesty and the meekness, the power and the humility, the glory and the poverty, all wrapped in one little babe. The only appropriate response was utterances of praise, body language bowed low, words acclaiming Him as God incarnate as they 'worshiped him.'

Then they 'opened their treasures,' a moment that has given delight to many a Christmas pageant. Many different theories have been developed over the hundreds of years that the devoted have reflected on this passage as to the meaning of these gifts. Matthew himself does not spell out their meaning. Often it is said that gold is given to represent Christ's kingliness, frankincense His priestliness, and myrrh as a prediction of His death. That may be so, or some other variation along the same lines, and yet also it is asking a lot of these Magi to know all these things at this point, or before they even arrived, about Jesus. Alternatively, these gifts may have simply been expensive, and easily portable for their journey, gifts that were appropriate as an honorable present to the King of Kings.

Then, another divine intervention in the lives of these Magi. They are warned in a dream not to go back to Herod, and so they slip his leash and go back to their own country by a different route.

Christmas is a time when the Christ-child still draws people from every nation, east and west, to come and worship. Worship by its nature is costly. We are centering our lives on God, not on ourselves, and to enjoy the One we worship, the focus of our attention and existence must be on that One that we do worship. Like the Magi, we must bow low and give the costly gift of our time, talent, and resources, as we 'worship Him' and so be 'overjoyed.'

*O Star of wonder, star of light*
*Star with royal beauty bright,*
*Westward leading, still proceeding*

*Guide us to Thy perfect light.*
*Glorious now behold Him arise*
*King and God and Sacrifice*
*Alleluia, Alleluia*
*Earth to heav'n replies.*

**'We Three Kings of Orient Are'** by John Henry Hopkins, 1857

# SOVEREIGN JOY

*When they had gone, an angel of the Lord appeared to Joseph in a dream. 'Get up,' he said, 'take the child and his mother and escape to Egypt. Stay there until I tell you, for Herod is going to search for the child to kill him.'*

*So he got up, took the child and his mother during the night and left for Egypt, where he stayed until the death of Herod. And so was fulfilled what the Lord had said through the prophet: 'Out of Egypt I called my son.'*
**(MATTHEW 2:13-15)**

It was a busy season for the angels, relatively rare as their appearances are in the rest of Scripture, packed now together in this seismic, earth-changing, heaven-revealing moment around the incarnation of God. The angel's instructions are clear: leave, 'get up,' and go with your family and 'escape to Egypt.' Lest such instruction be greeted with surprise and horror—they had hardly had a chance to get settled as a family, after all—the angel makes it clear the reason why. Herod is looking for the child, and his goal is evil: to kill the child. Jesus, born King, threatens Herod's kingdom, and Herod is enacting a policy as predictable as it is evil and pathetic. He will not succeed in his malevolent aims. In fact, they will stay in Egypt, Matthew tells us, until the death of Herod. It is not wise to oppose the Son of God and seek to kill Him. Herod would have done better to have submitted to this new-born King.

This move to Egypt made the young family refugees. They were far from home, living in a foreign country, having to become acclimated to foreign ways of doing things. How did they provide for themselves? Was Joseph's skill set as a carpenter sufficiently portable that he could ply a trade in Egypt and so look after his family? Where did they live? What sort of friendships and support could they find as they tried to become accustomed to their new role as parents, not to mention being parents of Jesus as they sought to fulfill the duties that had been entrusted to them?

It was a tall order, a difficult task. And yet, like everything in this world, but specifically here at this moment of fulfillment, it had a providential, and in this case specifically prophetic intentionality behind it. 'Out of Egypt I called my son.' The reference is not only to a particular Bible verse in the Old Testament, but also to the pattern of redemption of the Old Testament. The Old Testament story, in very broad brush strokes, is a story of God's covenant people going down to Egypt, then being called out of Egypt, and then being formed into a people under God's rule. It is clear from the story that they never managed to live up to that calling, and so now, God's true Son, Jesus Himself, is going to be the 'Son' that Israel never quite lived up to being. Jesus will live the perfect life and die the death, as our representative head, so that those who trust in Him can be rescued and in Him have the righteousness of God.

This story reminds us that God is sovereign over even our difficult family circumstances. But even more, it tells us that God is sovereign over all circumstances, all powers and authorities, to lead us to the true King Jesus.

*For lo! the days are hastening on,*
*By prophets seen of old,*
*When with the ever-circling years*
*Shall come the time foretold,*
*When the new heaven and earth shall own*
*The Prince of Peace, their King,*
*And the whole world send back the song*
*Which now the angels sing.*

**'It Came Upon the Midnight Clear'** by Edmund Hamilton Sears, 1849

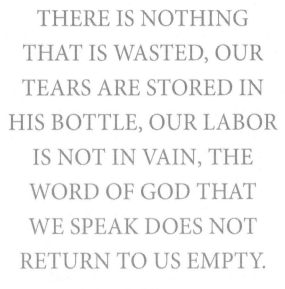

"

THERE IS NOTHING
THAT IS WASTED, OUR
TEARS ARE STORED IN
HIS BOTTLE, OUR LABOR
IS NOT IN VAIN, THE
WORD OF GOD THAT
WE SPEAK DOES NOT
RETURN TO US EMPTY.

(p.91)

# SIGNIFICANT JOY

*When Herod realized that he had been outwitted by the Magi, he was furious, and he gave orders to kill all the boys in Bethlehem and its vicinity who were two years old and under, in accordance with the time he had learned from the Magi. Then what was said through the prophet Jeremiah was fulfilled:*

*'A voice is heard in Ramah,*
  *weeping and great mourning,*
*Rachel weeping for her children*
  *and refusing to be comforted,*
*because they are no more.'* **(MATTHEW 2:16-18)**

Now we come to the saddest part of the story, at least at a human level. Herod is 'furious.' Imagine him flying into a rage. Those Magi fooled him! Well, he is left (in his own sick mind) with one other option. As he cannot determine exactly which child is being acclaimed as king, threatening his own throne and his dynasty, then he must kill the lot of them. He has learnt from the Magi the rough birthday of the child, and so he sweeps with a broad brush and will gather up into the grave all boys in the area of Bethlehem under two years old—he will kill them. He does not particularly want to do it, perhaps, but he reasons to himself that he must protect the crown, and you cannot make an omelet without breaking a few eggs.

In case we miss the immensity of the tragedy, Matthew quotes from Jeremiah. There is a voice heard in Ramah. Now, not the voice of the announcement of good news, but the uncontrollable weeping of a mother for her child. There is no comfort that can be given, 'refusing to be comforted.' 'Weeping and great mourning.'

Into such darkness, the light of Christmas shines. There is at Christmas hope for the hopeless, strength for the weary, comfort for the comfortless, joy for the downcast, and meaning for those suffering. That is the constant question of those in pain: why? There is a need to find an answer or at least a framework through which it can all be understood. You can put up with almost any how if you have a why. And Christ at Christmas provides for those 'weeping in Ramah' by giving them an eternal meaning that is all focused on the brilliant light of the Christ-child.

In Him, your life does have meaning. In Him, no life is wasted. In Him, there is a future and hope for all who trust in Him. There is nothing that is wasted, our tears are stored in His bottle, our labor is not in vain, the Word of God that we speak does not return to us empty.

It is this overcoming joy that is part of the miracle of Christmas. A person on the edge can come back from the edge and realize that each and every day was written before He lived it, and as painful as some of those days have been, they are not now without meaning or purpose or larger significance in the grand story of God and of His people.

*Chains shall He break, for the slave is our brother.*
*And in His name all oppression shall cease.*
*Sweet hymns of joy in grateful chorus raise we,*
*With all our hearts we praise His holy name.*
*Christ is the Lord! Then ever, ever praise we,*
*His power and glory ever more proclaim!*
*His power and glory ever more proclaim!*

**'O Holy Night'** by Adolph Adam, 1847

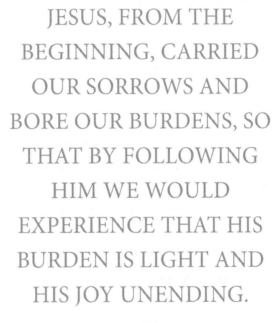

JESUS, FROM THE BEGINNING, CARRIED OUR SORROWS AND BORE OUR BURDENS, SO THAT BY FOLLOWING HIM WE WOULD EXPERIENCE THAT HIS BURDEN IS LIGHT AND HIS JOY UNENDING.

(p.95)

# REAL JOY

*After Herod died, an angel of the Lord appeared in a dream to Joseph in Egypt and said, 'Get up, take the child and his mother and go to the land of Israel, for those who were trying to take the child's life are dead.'*

*So he got up, took the child and his mother and went to the land of Israel. But when he heard that Archelaus was reigning in Judea in place of his father Herod, he was afraid to go there. Having been warned in a dream, he withdrew to the district of Galilee, and he went and lived in a town called Nazareth. So was fulfilled what was said through the prophets, that he would be called a Nazarene.* **(MATTHEW 2:19-23)**

Once more the Messianic little family is on the move, again in response to dreams, the first one to announce the death of Herod (known as the 'great') and then again to warn Joseph about the nefarious activities of Herod's son (known as Herod 'Archelaus'). In all this we can discern the sovereign care of our God over Joseph and Mary and the baby boy.

Our experiences of God's sovereign care may not be so direct—there is more angelic activity at this time in history than ever before or since—but though it is less direct in normal instances, it is no less real. God cares for His people, those who are in Christ, and defends them and protects them. There is no promise of being removed from all the ills of this world; indeed, Christ will pray that we not be taken out of this world but remain in this world—in the world but not of the world—to be a witness to Him in the midst of this life. But He who is in us is greater than He who is in the world, and God gives His people strength, wisdom, courage, and constantly weaves together the plots of their adversaries for the great good of His people and His own great glory. We are not told of Joseph's emotional state through all these changes of location. He was obedient, that is all we know, and it is enough.

Joseph heads to Galilee, to the North, to live in Nazareth, and Matthew tells us that this fulfills what the prophets said about Jesus being 'called a Nazarene.' What does Matthew mean by this? Probably Matthew has in mind that Jesus will experience derision in much the same way that others from Nazareth experienced derision. The prophets made it clear that the Messiah would not be accepted—a general theme in the Old Testament Scriptures—and would be mocked and beaten and even in the end crucified for our sins. This 'Nazarene'-like derision and rejection was a prophesied aspect of the Messiah's ministry and one that Jesus fulfilled. John's Gospel preserves the same idea when he records one of Jesus' early disciples, Nathanael, replying to the invitation to come and see Jesus by protesting, 'Nazareth! Can anything good come from there?' (John 1:46). Psalm 22 and Isaiah 53 are a couple of places where this theme of what Matthew calls Jesus' 'Nazarene' rejection is predicted in the Old Testament.

Once again, we find that the real Christmas story is, while indelibly 'sweet,' one whose 'light' shines against 'darkness.' Sometimes people find Christmas to be so unreal that it cannot speak to them in their rejection. Jesus, from the beginning, carried our sorrows and bore our burdens, so that by following Him we would experience that His burden is light and His joy unending. Would you entrust to this Christ-child your sorrows today so that in Him you might find the true Christmas joy of life forevermore?

> *No more let sins and sorrows grow,*
> *Nor thorns infest the ground;*
> *He comes to make His blessings flow*

*Far as the curse is found,*
*Far as the curse is found,*
*Far as, far as, the curse is found.*

**'Joy to the World'** by Isaac Watts, 1719

# GLORIOUS JOY

*And the child grew and became strong; he was filled with wisdom, and the grace of God was on him.*
**(LUKE 2:40)**

Having covered most of the traditional 'birth narrative' already in our leading up to Christmas, it feels a little flat to hear about the 'child growing and becoming strong.' One of our family traditions growing up was always eating 'shepherd's pie' on Christmas Eve because (we heard half-ironically) the shepherds were watching their flocks that evening! To read on December 24 about the child 'growing and becoming strong,' you might think 'where are the shepherds?'!

But on this Christmas Eve, this brief description from Luke emphasizes what sometimes the nascent warm glow of the nativity can hide behind its sentimentality in our various pageant traditions. It emphasizes the humanity of Jesus. John, in his famous 'Prologue,' emphasizes this humanity in his own way by talking boldly of the Word becoming 'flesh' (John 1:14), real flesh and blood and bone. Similarly, in a different way, and later in the story, Luke tells us that the child grew and became strong. Jesus was subject to physical normal human development. The wonder of the incarnation, the humility of God, is perhaps never more extraordinary than in the fact that the Son of God had to learn how to walk and talk and run.

However, even from this human perspective the observant neighbor would have noticed something incandescent about the Christ. He was 'filled with wisdom.' It is not often that you hear of a 'child' being called 'wise.' That is normally a descriptor that is won through hard fought, often painful experience, appended to a life well lived, and ending its final leg of the race. An old man may be wise; how often can that be said of a child? But it was true of Christ, and abundantly so: He was 'filled with wisdom,' this Word Incarnate. What is more, the same observant neighbor would have noted the 'grace of God was on him.' God favored Him and loved him, and the favor of God was 'on him' in some way that was apparent to those who knew Him.

Elsewhere from Luke, and from the other Gospel authors, we know that this Christ-child is far more than a human child, but He is never less than a human child, even so at this moment of His birth and in this development as He 'grew and became strong.'

The sheer humility of God in becoming incarnate is hard to fathom. Paul tried to describe it in Philippians 2:6-7 (ESV), 'though he was in the form of God, did not count equality with God a thing to be grasped, but emptied himself, by taking the form of a servant, being born in the likeness of men.' He was the very likeness of humanity, growing and becoming strong, and yet also the fullness of deity.

Mystery all, that for us God Himself would condescend to stoop so low to lift us so high.

> *The heavenly Babe*
> *You there shall find*
> *To human view displayed*
> *And meanly wrapped*
> *In swathing bands*
> *And in a manger laid*
> *And in a manger laid.*
>
> *All glory be to*
> *God on high*
> *And to the earth be peace;*
> *Goodwill henceforth*
> *From heaven to men*

*Begin and never cease*
*Begin and never cease!*

**'While Shepherds Watched Their Flocks by Night'**
by Nahum Tate, 1703

# ENDLESS JOY

*For God so loved the world that he gave his one and only Son, that whoever believes in him shall not perish but have eternal life.* **(JOHN 3:16)**

What better summary of the meaning of Christmas could there be than Christ's own summary of the significance of that first Christmas Gift, and its resulting life, death, and resurrection!

When I was on the mission field—my very brief foray into residential mission work and a slightly longer ensuing oversight-coordinating role of some pioneer mission opportunities in the same region of the world—a team member of ours from Denmark said that the Danish Christians called this verse 'the little Bible.' Whether or not that is true, and I have no reason to doubt it (perhaps Danish friends will write and tell us otherwise!), it is a great explanation of the significance of this very well-known verse. In its brief statement, it encompasses a Tardis-like universe of meaning, bigger on the inside than it is apparently on the outside.

It tells us that God loves the world. In John, the 'world' does not primarily mean the world as in the whole vast population of the globe, though surely the cosmos in that sense is in view too, but the world as in 'the world in rebellion.' What is extraordinary about this statement, then, is not that Jesus loves *so many* people but that He loves *such bad* people. In that sense, then, Christmas and its true significance can never really be grasped without a right perspective on the extraordinary love of God for you and for me, bad people as we are. The heart is wicked, deceitful above all, and its wickedness is only surpassed by its blindness to that wickedness. And yet, God 'loved the world'! Oh, glorious thought!

God's love is not passive, but active, and it overflows into action. He 'gave his one and only Son.' Passing on by with 'deliberate neglect' (as I heard Alistair Begg once call this technique), not delving into the intertextual or theological niceties of the grammar of this great incarnation claim of the eternal generation of God the Son, we can say that this 'only' Son is God eternal, and God much loved. God's love—Father, Son and Holy Spirit—is so bountiful it overflows into a Christmas morning Gift, a Gift beyond parallel ('sans parallel' as the French say) and beyond marvel.

The Gift is not passive, but also its blessings are not automatically received. This Gift requires opening. There is no point looking at the gift beneath the Christmas tree and leaving it unopened, thinking to ourselves what a beautiful gift, how nice and shiny.

Sometimes we are tempted to do that with gifts we receive, knowing by experience that the anticipation is often better than the receiving. And sometimes we mouth inglorious platitudes of polite pleasure at the opening of the gift to well-meaning relatives, knowing full well that we would have preferred something slightly different than what was given, even if also we know the point is the giver and the heart behind the gift, not the actual physical item itself.

But this Gift is never disappointing. It cannot be. It not only represents the divine heart of the Giver, it is itself the divine Gift. There is no reason to stand back and wait. Go on and open it! 'Believe'!

And if we do, then, to use one of John's favorite words in his writings in the New Testament, 'life' is the result. We will not 'perish,' meaning the eternal judgment and condemnation of hell, but instead we will have life, the fullness of life, and 'life eternal.' This 'life' is such that it overwhelmingly continues into a boundless eternity.

With all this on offer on Christmas, then whatever else is true—whatever else has happened, whatever else has been said, whoever else we may miss or wish were here, or whatever regrets we may have—then we have this truth, this 'little Bible,' invested in the little babe who tells us, 'silently pleading,' of a joy without ending, and a life forever.

*Joy to the world, the Lord is come!*
*Let earth receive her King;*
*Let every heart prepare Him room,*
*And Heaven and nature sing,*
*And Heaven and nature sing,*
*And Heaven, and Heaven, and nature sing.*

**'Joy to the World'** by Isaac Watts, 1719